Original title:
The Softness of Love's Embrace

Copyright © 2025 Creative Arts Management OÜ
All rights reserved.

Author: Milo Harrington
ISBN HARDBACK: 978-3-69081-339-6
ISBN PAPERBACK: 978-3-69081-835-3

Whispers of Gentle Hearts

In a world so wide and vast,
Two hearts found joy, not outcast.
They giggle softly, side by side,
Like two ducks on a wild ride.

With snuggles sweet and silly grins,
They dance like worms in a tin of bins.
A playful poke, a gentle tease,
Spreading laughter like a warm breeze.

Caresses in Moonlight

Underneath the glowing moon,
They play like kids, not stopping soon.
A tickle here, a playful shove,
Their laughter sings, the song of love.

As stars peep down with a twinkling wink,
They share goofy looks, no time to think.
With stolen kisses on the cheek,
The night is bright, the future sleek.

Embraced by Twilight's Glow

In twilight's glow, they toss and tease,
Like two squirrels chasing a breeze.
A ghostly hug, a poke surprise,
A whirlwind mix of love and pies.

Their hearts beat fast, a rhythmic thump,
Like bunnies who've found a perfect hump.
With laughter light as summer air,
They throw confetti, no single care.

Caresses in Moonlight

Underneath the glowing moon,
They play like kids, not stopping soon.
A tickle here, a playful shove,
Their laughter sings, the song of love.

As stars peep down with a twinkling wink,
They share goofy looks, no time to think.
With stolen kisses on the cheek,
The night is bright, the future sleek.

Embraced by Twilight's Glow

In twilight's glow, they toss and tease,
Like two squirrels chasing a breeze.
A ghostly hug, a poke surprise,
A whirlwind mix of love and pies.

Their hearts beat fast, a rhythmic thump,
Like bunnies who've found a perfect hump.
With laughter light as summer air,
They throw confetti, no single care.

Tender Echoes of Affection

They hug like bears on a sunny day,
With giggles bouncing, come what may.
A fumble here, a syrupy kiss,
Every moment feels like bliss.

Silly faces, each one a treat,
Two clumsy puppies dancing on feet.
In their world, joy is the aim,
And love's a wild and playful game.

The Nest of Shared Silences

In a cozy nook, we sit and stare,
Counting crumbs scattered everywhere.
You snack on chips, I sip some tea,
In perfect silence, just you and me.

A funny face and a goofy grin,
You giggle hard as I munch my skin.
We trade our laughs like silly toys,
In our quiet nest, we're just two boys.

A wink from you, my heart takes flight,
As shadows dance in the soft moonlight.
We chuckle at everything we see,
In shared moments, we feel so free.

With every sigh, a thousand jokes,
We're two old socks, but we're happy folks.
In the soft glow of our funny chat,
I love you more than my favorite hat.

Harmonies in Gentle Touch

When you poke me, I can't help but laugh,
Your silly antics, a warm giraffe.
We sway together, like trees in line,
With soft touches that feel quite divine.

Your tickles spark a sparkly dance,
A shared glance makes my heart take a chance.
With mousey noises, we prance around,
In our own world, joyfully unbound.

A quiet chuckle, a nudge with a poke,
You say, "What's up?" as I crack a joke.
In our duet of laughter's sweet song,
We find a rhythm where we both belong.

Here's to the whispers, the giggles we share,
In this sweet chaos, we happily dare.
Our silly love makes the world seem bright,
With every chuckle, you're my delight.

Folds of Warm Embrace

In cozy corners we both snuggle,
Like two lost socks in a laundry struggle.
Your laugh's a tickle, my heart's a dance,
We trip on love, lost in a trance.

Chasing each other around the room,
Dodging dust bunnies, avoiding gloom.
A pie in the face can spark a grin,
In this game of hearts, we both win.

Fruitful Gardens of Harmony

In a garden bright with wacky blooms,
We plant our dreams amidst the fumes.
Giggling gnomes and squirrels in suits,
Love grows wild among the fruits.

With honeyed smiles and cheeky winks,
We water hope with silly drinks.
A picnic spread, all a-dither,
Each bite brings laughter, love grows thicker.

Shadows of Gentle Affection

In the twilight, your shadow creeps,
You trip on your shoelace, laughter leaps.
We dodge the stars, they give a wink,
In this silly dusk, we just think.

Playing tag with flickering lights,
Chasing giggles through the nights.
Your silly faces, my heart's delight,
Together we shine, like planets so bright.

Fruitful Gardens of Harmony

In a garden bright with wacky blooms,
We plant our dreams amidst the fumes.
Giggling gnomes and squirrels in suits,
Love grows wild among the fruits.

With honeyed smiles and cheeky winks,
We water hope with silly drinks.
A picnic spread, all a-dither,
Each bite brings laughter, love grows thicker.

Shadows of Gentle Affection

In the twilight, your shadow creeps,
You trip on your shoelace, laughter leaps.
We dodge the stars, they give a wink,
In this silly dusk, we just think.

Playing tag with flickering lights,
Chasing giggles through the nights.
Your silly faces, my heart's delight,
Together we shine, like planets so bright.

Kissed by the Quiet Universe

In midnight whispers, we both float,
Your sock puppet says, 'Vote for the goat!'
We search for constellations so wide,
With marshmallow stars, we giggle and glide.

The moon chuckles, the stars chime in,
Our quiet antics, a joyful spin.
In this cosmic dance, we find our place,
Hand in hand, we embrace the grace.

Lullaby of Two Souls

In the twilight's giggle, we sway,
Like jelly beans dancing, come what may.
Your snore's a melody, offbeat, off cue,
Yet in every note, I still love you.

Pillow fights raging, we laugh and we clash,
Feathers a-flying, what a comic splash!
Your silly grin, as you dip and you dive,
In this wobbly waltz, we feel so alive.

Gentle Breezes of Belonging

We shared a sandwich, stacked way too high,
Ketchup and mustard, oh what a pie!
You wore my bowtie, I sported your hat,
Together we're goofy, like two friendly cats.

In our cozy corner, we chuckle and cheer,
Your laughter's contagious, it fills me with beer—
Well, soda, I mean, but let's not be coy,
With you by my side, I'm the world's luckiest boy.

The Warmth Between Us

In blankets piled high, we snuggle and squeeze,
Your feet are so cold, it's like winter's tease.
Yet I find it charming, your frozen little toes,
A pair of warm socks? No one quite knows!

We dance in the kitchen, twirling around,
The dog joins the party, what silliness found!
Your apron is stained with spaghetti and cheese,
But in this mad kitchen, we do as we please.

Petals on a Quiet Breeze

Our garden's a riot, flowers gone wild,
You named a petunia, and I just smiled.
With each little joke, like daisies we bloom,
Entwined in the laughter that fills up the room.

The wind carries whispers, our secrets so sweet,
In this big flower bed, our hearts skip a beat.
With you, every moment's a soft, silly spree,
Like petals on breezes, it's just you and me.

Waves of Gentle Reassurance

In a sea of pillows, we float with glee,
Our giggles echo like waves, you see.
Snuggled up tight, there's a rhythm in play,
Like a soft surf, washing worries away.

Popcorn fights burst, as laughter takes flight,
Caught in a whirlwind, oh what a sight!
Like jellybeans tossed, our joy knows no bounds,
A playful embrace where pure love resounds.

Petals on a Quiet Breeze

Our garden's a riot, flowers gone wild,
You named a petunia, and I just smiled.
With each little joke, like daisies we bloom,
Entwined in the laughter that fills up the room.

The wind carries whispers, our secrets so sweet,
In this big flower bed, our hearts skip a beat.
With you, every moment's a soft, silly spree,
Like petals on breezes, it's just you and me.

Waves of Gentle Reassurance

In a sea of pillows, we float with glee,
Our giggles echo like waves, you see.
Snuggled up tight, there's a rhythm in play,
Like a soft surf, washing worries away.

Popcorn fights burst, as laughter takes flight,
Caught in a whirlwind, oh what a sight!
Like jellybeans tossed, our joy knows no bounds,
A playful embrace where pure love resounds.

Ballet of Heartbeats

We pirouette round in our cozy nook,
In this dance of rhythms, I'm hooked on your look.
With every misstep, a chuckle we share,
Two left feet prance, no troubles to bear!

Your heart taps a tune that I know in my soul,
Together we whirl, that's our ultimate goal.
Spinning through life, with a playful twirl,
In this dance of two, oh how our love swirls!

Mellow Serenades of Belonging

Under a blanket fort, we grasp at the light,
Soft serenades echo, everything feels right.
With silly voices, we sing a sweet song,
As the world melts away, it's where we belong.

Like pancakes flipped high, our laughter erupts,
A syrupy spill, in our bond it's all wrapped.
Sipping on cocoa, each sip feels divine,
Our whispers like candy, oh how we entwine!

Tapestry of Tender Encounters

In cozy corners, we weave tales of delight,
Each thread a chuckle, as day turns to night.
Your snorts and your sighs are my favorite of sounds,
A woven tapestry where affection abounds.

Like candy canes tangled, we're caught in a tie,
Each hug is a patch, oh my, oh my!
With every bright moment, colors collide,
In this tapestry of love, we take great pride.

A Mosaic of Tender Whispers

In a kitchen filled with flour,
A cat thinks it's a flower.
Whiskers twitching, tiny paws,
Perfect chaos gives us pause.

A pair of socks in disarray,
That question, 'Did you wear them today?'
With laughter shared, our hearts will bloom,
In love's warm, cozy, scented room.

Every chuckle, every tease,
A dance of joy, as sweet as cheese.
In every wink, a world we trust,
Together, wanderlust and rust.

Underneath a starlit gaze,
We chuckle at our silly ways.
Here's to whispers, warm and bright,
In the shadows, our hearts take flight.

Fleeting Glances of Forever

You stole my fries, I stole your heart,
In this game, we're both so smart.
With every bite, unexpected fun,
It's a love story, always on the run.

The way you grin when you tease,
Making socks dance, a gentle breeze.
A pillow fight, a feathery glow,
In our bizarre love, thoughts overflow.

I trip on air, you catch my fall,
Your laughter echoes, a comforting call.
With silly quirks, our quirks combine,
In these fleeting glances, forever shine.

Over spilled drinks and broken chairs,
We patch it up with tender snares.
In the chaos, love's sweet refrain,
We laugh together through all the pain.

Pillows of Trust

You dream of flying through the blue,
While I just dream of nachos too.
Our mornings start with sleepy grins,
A little chaos, where love begins.

Pillow forts and cuddly naps,
Silly hats and happy claps.
With every little snort and sigh,
We weave our laughter, you and I.

In tickle fights, we wrestle away,
Goodnight kisses lead to the day.
Under blankets, we share our fears,
Wrapped in dreams, mixed with our cheers.

Through tangled sheets and giddy spins,
Our love's a dance where everyone wins.
In whispered jokes and secret plans,
We build our world with silly fans.

Softly Spoken Signs

With a wink and a playful shove,
I know you feel that spark of love.
A secret code we both can read,
In every glance, we plant a seed.

The breakfast chaos, sunny-side up,
You spill the juice, I bring the cup.
With syrup drips and messy hair,
Our morning giggles fill the air.

You snore a song, sweet and profound,
While I plot ways to tease you round.
A silly dance in the kitchen light,
With softly spoken signs, we ignite.

When you misplace your favorite hat,
I wear it proudly, just like that.
In every laugh, a special ring,
Together, we embrace everything.

Enveloping Wings of Affection

Your hugs feel like clouds, I must confess,
Where laughter and silliness mingle and bless.
We dance in the kitchen, it's all quite absurd,
You trip on the rug, oh, who needs a bird?

Though bills are a drag, we still have our fun,
With your silly jokes, the day's never done.
Your giggles like bubbles, they float in the air,
Who's serious now? We've not a care!

Echoes of Mutual Tenderness

In the morning light, we wrestle for sheets,
Your cold feet attack me, oh what funny feats!
With coffee in hand and a wink in your eye,
We laugh at the cats, they're the spies in the sky.

Your eyes are like stars, yet they squint with glee,
When we try to dance, it's a sight to see.
You trip on your toes, I can't help but chime,
Love's got some quirks, but oh, isn't it prime?

A Symphony of Quiet Devotion

In our tiny bubble, the world feels so vast,
We sing off-key songs, raising questions of class.
Your snoring is music, a soft serenade,
With every weird note, my heart feels the trade.

We shuffle through life, in slippers and shorts,
With snacks made for kings, we'll hold our retorts.
Your side-eye's a treasure, your smirk's quite the show,
Together we're goofy, just thought you should know!

Cascading Kisses of Closeness

With seconds to spare, you swipe my last fry,
I feign a big frown, but I can't help but sigh.
Your silly attempts to be sweet and sincere,
Leave me rolling with laughter, oh my dear!

Each peck on the cheek, like a game we both play,
You make me a pizza, then toss it away.
Our evenings are chaos, filled with playful delight,
In this wacky dance, love feels just right!

Feathers on the Breeze of Passion

In a room full of kittens, we tumble and twirl,
Your socks are mismatched—a colorful swirl.
We dance like a buffet's delightfully strange,
With a sprinkle of chaos as we rearrange.

Your laugh is my music, slightly off-key,
As you chase after crumbs that were spilled by the bee.
In this circus of giggles, I find my own place,
With you, every mishap's a reason to grace.

Caressing the Dawn of Togetherness

Morning light peeks in like a cheeky cat,
Your hair's a disaster—a sight to combat.
Yet as you brew coffee, your smile's divine,
I swear, that first sip tastes like you and fine wine.

We stumble through breakfast—toast flies with style,
Jam's on the ceiling—oh, what a big smile!
In our flour-filled kitchen, I'll dance with a spoon,
While you do the cha-cha with the old vacuum.

Serenity in You

With you, even silence can giggle and grin,
Our pet goldfish flops as if he's joining in.
In the glow of our laughter, simplicity reigns,
As we play silly games in the softest of chains.

Your quirky dance moves give the cat a rash,
As we try to compete in the classic 'mad dash.'
Yet through all the antics and giggles anew,
I'm serenely grateful—in chaos, it's you.

Traces of Love's Embrace

Like fingerprints left on a frosty window,
Our love's a wild picnic where memories glow.
With sandwiches flying and ants on parade,
We laugh as they march through the crumbs that we've laid.

Your snorts and your chuckles, a charming delight,
Like a balloon filled with giggles—oh, what a sight!
Though sticky and messy, our hearts intertwine,
In silliness wrapped, your laughter is mine.

The Embrace of Starlit Eyes

Under the glow of the moonlight,
You dance like a clumsy cat.
Your laughter fills the cool air,
I trip, but you just laugh back.

In your gaze, I find a spark,
Like fireflies trapped in a jar.
You whisper sweet silly things,
Like how you'd run off to the stars.

Each hug is a gentle tumble,
Wrapped in a blanket of care.
But somehow I miscalculate,
Falling like I'm walking on air.

When we share a bowl of popcorn,
You toss yours right at my nose.
It's a game of silly nonsense,
But love is the punchline that glows.

Charms of Gentle Promises

Your wink is a charming riddle,
A magic trick in plain view.
We giggle at all our secrets,
Like kids who just broke the rules.

You promised me the moon and stars,
But settled for an old sock.
In laughter, we twirl in circles,
Made silly by that tick-tock.

Every sweet word's a warm cuddle,
Wrapped up in bright, goofy jokes.
You call me your silly penguin,
With silly waddles and pokes.

In a world of funny moments,
We create our goofy ways.
With laughter as our secret code,
Love's charm never frays.

Starlit Pathways of Us

We wander through fields of crickets,
You trip on a patch of grass.
But when you fall, it's with laughter,
Like a balloon that loses gas.

With each step, we chase the night,
Searching for giggles and fun.
You say your shadow's your twin now,
And we'll race 'til we both run.

We draw silly maps in the air,
Guided by giggles and sighs.
The path is paved with bright memories,
Under the glow of starry skies.

In the garden of nightime blooms,
You plant jokes that start to sprout.
In this silly race of moments,
Love giggles, we dance about.

A Dreamscape in Soft Colors

In a swirl of pastel whispers,
You dream in shades of delight.
I'm the clown with floppy shoes,
And you giggle at my height.

We paint our world with wild colors,
Your brush is a ticklish hand.
Each stroke is a sweet adventure,
In this make-believe land.

We bounce on clouds of marshmallow,
And dive into puddles of glee.
Each dream's just a wink away,
Where we can both feel free.

As the stars shine like bright candy,
Every moment's a sweet breeze.
In this whimsical dreamscape,
Love is the joy that never leaves.

Embrace of Gentle Cascades

In a world of fluffy clouds,
We giggle at the bounce,
Each hug a soft cascade,
Falling with a joyful pounce.

With every silly squeeze,
We're like marshmallows in flight,
Laughter bursts like bubbles,
In the glow of moonlit night.

Tickles travel like wild streams,
Unexpected, yet so sweet,
Like a candy-coated dream,
Or dancing to our own heartbeat.

In this cascade of laughter,
We splash in joy's warm sea,
Holding on just a bit tighter,
You and your silly me.

Sunlit Paths of Togetherness

On sunny days we prance and play,
With each step, we trip and fall,
Laughter echoes through the rays,
As we make a grand light brawl.

You're sunshine in my cup of tea,
Spilling sweetness, oh so bright,
Like a puppy on a spree,
Bounding joyfully in delight.

We skip and hop on flower paths,
While butterflies take a chance,
Funny faces, quirky laughs,
In our happy little dance.

Sunbeams tickle while we roam,
Finding treasures in the air,
Every misstep feels like home,
In this wild, playful affair.

A Nest of Consolation

In the cuddle of a tossled bed,
Pillow forts that have no rules,
Your snoring sounds like music, said,
To soothe the silliest of fools.

Nestled tight in blankets warm,
We're like two peas in a pod,
Bumbling through our goofy charm,
Finding peace in every nod.

Cookies crumble as we laugh,
Each crumb a tiny delight,
Sharing tales of our past gaffes,
Chasing shadows in the night.

In this nest, all woes dissolve,
Wrapped in giggles, kisses too,
With every silly problem solved,
Finding comfort just with you.

Hearts Aglow in Silken Touch

Your fingertips weave silly tales,
As they dance along my skin,
In this moment, laughter sails,
As our playful hearts begin.

Like kittens rolling on the floor,
Our feelings glide, oh so bright,
Every brush, we want some more,
Giggling till we see the light.

In the fabric of our sway,
Threads of joy combine and twine,
Your touch ignites a funny play,
Rainbows spark in every line.

With whispers wrapped in velvety hugs,
We spark like fireworks at dawn,
Amidst the chaos, warm and snug,
In this embrace, we carry on.

Subtle Currents of Fondness

In a cozy nook, two hearts collide,
Hand in hand, let the giggles glide.
With a wink and a nudge, they tease and play,
Over spilled popcorn, they laugh the day away.

Whispers of mischief dance in the air,
As silly jokes float without a care.
Their secrets shared, like jellybeans sweet,
In this colorful chaos, their worlds complete.

Sighs Beneath the Starlit Sky

Underneath the stars, two dorks convene,
Counting the constellations, like a movie scene.
With a laugh so loud, they shake the night,
While a cat sneezes, causing sheer delight.

A wink and a nudge, with a playful sigh,
They ponder if aliens watch from up high.
With the moon as a witness, they dream and scheme,
Plotting adventures straight out of a dream.

Embracing the Sweetness Within

In the kitchen, chaos, a floury scene,
Baking mishaps turn into a routine.
With cupcakes exploding and icing gone wild,
They laugh 'til they cry, like a giddy child.

Muffin mayhem becomes a delight,
As they wear aprons splattered in white.
With every sweet morsel they taste and hold,
Their joy doubles, worth more than gold.

Gentle Hands, Kindred Spirits

Walking in sync, they trip on a shoe,
A skirmish of laughter as they tumble anew.
With hands clasped tight, they dodge a small dog,
In this dance of glee, they leap like a frog.

Side by side, they fumble and sway,
Creating a ruckus in their own quirky way.
With hearts wide open, they stumble and grin,
In a friendship that feels like a cheeky win.

Threads of Comfort in a Chaotic World

In a closet full of chaos,
My socks are out of sync.
Yet when you hug me tightly,
I forget the kitchen sink.

A blender hums a tune,
With fruit that sings out loud.
Your laughter breaks the gloom,
We dance, a little proud.

The dog steals all the treats,
Then gives a guilty glance.
You shake your head in wonder,
Can we have one more chance?

With you, life's a circus,
Filled with clowns and flair.
In the chaos, I find peace,
Wrapped in love's sweet care.

Embrace of Timeless Understanding

Amidst the pots and pans,
Your smile does shine bright.
You understand my quirks,
Even when I'm not right.

With every silly joke,
You laugh until you snort.
In the mess of daily life,
You're my favorite sport.

When socks go missing fast,
And pants might have a stain,
Your eyes hold all the answers,
Through laughter or through pain.

In our stylish chaos,
With passion, we ignite.
Each hug is an adventure,
In our funny love fight.

Whispers of Warmth

Your whispers fill the air,
Like tickles in the breeze.
Every word is music,
Bringing me to my knees.

Bubble baths and giggles,
Spilled wine on the couch.
Life's a messy canvas,
Each brushstroke shows the ouch.

In the kitchen, we collide,
With flour flying high.
You sneak a kiss and wink,
As cookies start to fry.

Our love's a playful tease,
With jokes that never end.
In laughter's lively dance,
You always are my friend.

Tender Threads of Affection

In the fabric of our days,
We weave with joyful cheer.
Your quirks and silly faces,
Are what I hold so dear.

The laundry's like a puzzle,
With colors all a-blend.
Yet tangled in your laughter,
Is where my heart will mend.

With ice cream splattered smiles,
And pillow fights at night,
Every moment spent with you,
Turns chaos into light.

Through life's delightful mess,
We cherish every thread.
In this comedic tapestry,
With you, I feel well-fed.

Radiance in the Twilight

In twilight's glow, we laugh and play,
Your silly dance makes night feel gay.
With wobbly knees, we sway like trees,
I trip over shadows, you giggle with ease.

We twirl like fireflies, all aglow,
Your jokes are bright, a radiant show.
Each chuckle bounces, a light-hearted song,
In our twilight world, we simply belong.

Cradled in Kindness

Wrapped up snug in blankets tight,
You snore like a bear, oh what a sight!
I nudge you gently, just to tease,
You grumble back, always so at ease.

Your goofy grin, my sleepy friend,
With laughter, we giggle, never to end.
In kindness' cradle, we make quite a pair,
Snuggling together, without a care.

The Tender Nest of Us

In a nest of pillows, we squish and squeeze,
You call it a fortress, I call it a tease.
With popcorn flying and laughter so near,
We're two little birds, chirping without fear.

Your silly antics, they make me sigh,
Like a clumsy owl, you can't help but fly.
In this tender nest, we play our best parts,
Crafting our moments, woven with hearts.

Feathers of Intimacy

Meandering through dreams, we softly collide,
Feathers are scattered, taking us for a ride.
Your pillow talk, so weird and funny,
Makes midnight echoes feel oh-so-honey.

As pillows engage in a feathery fight,
We laugh like kids, until morning light.
In this joyful chaos, our hearts do blend,
Creating a bond that never will end.

Embracing the Gentle Dawn

When morning light starts to creep,
We laugh away the need for sleep.
Your snoring like a gentle tune,
I wonder if it's night or noon.

With sunlight dancing on your face,
I nudge you in a playful chase.
We tumble through the blankets tight,
Like puppies finding joy in light.

The coffee spills in such a mess,
You laugh so hard, I must confess.
We're tangled in our silly fight,
Two goofy stars in morning light.

Caress of Heartstrings

Your ticklish toes, they find my side,
Like rabbits hopping, we can't hide.
A poke, a jab, a playful tease,
You set my heart on a funny breeze.

Our laughter bounces off the walls,
While clumsy dancing makes us fall.
You step on toes, I trip on air,
Who knew love could be such a dare?

With every wink and goofy grin,
Our hearts are tied, a joyful win.
In silly dances, we embrace,
Life's a circus, oh what a place!

Comfort in Every Curve

Curved like a pretzel, oh so fine,
We wrap around like spaghetti twine.
In cozy nooks, we share a sigh,
Your elbow poking my eye's goodbye.

We giggle as we spill the beans,
About our weirdest nighttime dreams.
A fortress built of pillows tall,
The ultimate comfort, an epic brawl.

With snacks and jokes and movies too,
We cuddle close, just me and you.
Beneath a blanket, we create,
Our fortress of silly love, so great!

Silken Shadows of Togetherness

In shadows soft, we hide and peek,
Like cats that plot and scheming sneak.
Your hand swipes at the feathered bits,
While I prepare for playful hits.

We chase the moonlight, hand in hand,
In this funny, fantastical land.
The silken sheets play hide and seek,
As giggles dance, I feel the peak.

With every tickle, every tease,
We find our rhythm, our hearts at ease.
In whispering dusk, our spirits soar,
This oddball love, I can't ignore!

Flavor of a Shared Breath

When you take a breath near me,
I giggle like I drank a bee.
Your whispers tickle, oh so sweet,
Like candy floss, a funny treat.

Our laughter bubbles in the air,
Your loving gaze, a playful stare.
We share a sigh, a silly dance,
In gusts of joy, our hearts prance.

The scent of cookies in the breeze,
Your laughter makes the world freeze.
Together we create a rhyme,
Breath by breath, we measure time.

With each exhale, a hint of glee,
In your embrace, I'm wild and free.
The flavor of that sudden smile,
Makes all my worries disappear for a while.

Sparks in a Serene Universe

Twinkling stars up in the night,
You wink, I chuckle with delight.
In cosmic jokes, we find our glow,
As silly dreams in galas flow.

Your hands create a stellar dance,
With each touch, I lose my chance.
Orbiting in your silly cheer,
We laugh until the world is clear.

Stars collide like our bright laughs,
In nebulae of sweet mishaps.
The universe finds us a pair,
Dancing through space without a care.

In the vastness, just you and me,
We're comets flying wild and free.
In this serenity, we spark and shine,
With humor that feels truly divine.

Veils of Affectionate Moments

Hiding behind curtains of lace,
You peek and make a funny face.
In every veil, a mystery lies,
Your playful grin ignites the skies.

Moments wrapped in sweet disguise,
Like little jokes and silly pies.
You throw a pillow, laughing loud,
In our house, love wears a shroud.

Every glance is a teasing fight,
In our embrace, we feel just right.
Wrapped in jokes, like a cozy quilt,
In this warmth, our troubles wilt.

Soft embraces and silly sighs,
Our laughter dances, never shy.
Every moment, a layer we peel,
In the folds of affection, we feel.

Sparks in a Serene Universe

Twinkling stars up in the night,
You wink, I chuckle with delight.
In cosmic jokes, we find our glow,
As silly dreams in galas flow.

Your hands create a stellar dance,
With each touch, I lose my chance.
Orbiting in your silly cheer,
We laugh until the world is clear.

Stars collide like our bright laughs,
In nebulae of sweet mishaps.
The universe finds us a pair,
Dancing through space without a care.

In the vastness, just you and me,
We're comets flying wild and free.
In this serenity, we spark and shine,
With humor that feels truly divine.

Veils of Affectionate Moments

Hiding behind curtains of lace,
You peek and make a funny face.
In every veil, a mystery lies,
Your playful grin ignites the skies.

Moments wrapped in sweet disguise,
Like little jokes and silly pies.
You throw a pillow, laughing loud,
In our house, love wears a shroud.

Every glance is a teasing fight,
In our embrace, we feel just right.
Wrapped in jokes, like a cozy quilt,
In this warmth, our troubles wilt.

Soft embraces and silly sighs,
Our laughter dances, never shy.
Every moment, a layer we peel,
In the folds of affection, we feel.

Sweet Tides of Connection

Like waves that crash with playful glee,
You splash your charm right over me.
Riding tides of laughter and fun,
Together we're the perfect run.

In the surf of our joyful spree,
You make the ocean feel like tea.
With every splash, our spirits rise,
In this sea, love never lies.

We float on currents of sweet cheer,
A loveboat sailing without fear.
Your funny jokes are seafoam bright,
Guiding us through the ocean's light.

Riding waves, we frolic and glide,
In this adventure, let's not hide.
With every tide, our hearts discover,
The joy we make, like waves that hover.

Hush of Heartbeats

In quiet corners, hearts collide,
Like jellybeans, they bounce and slide.
With every thump, they seem to giggle,
In a rhythm soft that makes one wiggle.

A whispered thought, a silly grin,
Like kittens sneaking out to spin.
Each pulse, a secret, can't be caught,
Two hearts in sync, tangled in thought.

Serenity's Gentle Hold

Like marshmallows in a cocoa mug,
Together we make a snug little hug.
Each laugh's a puff, a bubble burst,
In moments of calm, how sweetly we thirst.

A dance of sighs, pirouettes in air,
With tangled socks and wild bed hair.
To snuggle close, a joy so fine,
Like finding pennies that really shine.

A Dance of Vulnerable Souls

In pajamas soft, we twirl and sway,
Like penguins on ice, a wobbly display.
With each misstep, we burst in cheer,
A tango of clumsiness, no hint of fear.

Two hearts will trip and tumble about,
As laughter spills, we dance without doubt.
In this silly ballet of hearts on a spree,
We twirl like crazy, just you and me.

Warm Embers on a Winter's Night

Under covers, a fortress we build,
Tales of warmth, our cups are filled.
With goofy grins and marshmallow dreams,
We toast our hearts, or so it seems.

By crackling fires, we plot and scheme,
Who stole the cookies? A laugh, a beam!
In cozy nooks where worries take flight,
We share our secrets, both silly and bright.

Emotions in Gentle Ripples

In the pond of hearts, I toss a stone,
It ripples out loud, making love known.
Frogs join the choir, a hilarious croak,
Splashing around like a clumsy bloke.

We giggle like kids in a rain-drenched play,
Dancing in puddles, come what may.
With each little plop, our laughter expands,
Like fish giving high-fives with slippery hands.

Emotions tumble, a silly parade,
On the float of affection, quirky and spayed.
Love's a weird ride, a goofy old clown,
With a big red nose that can't settle down.

Yet in this frolic, we find our charm,
Wrapped in our quirks, oh, isn't it warm?
Through the silliness, our hearts conjoin,
In the ripples of joy, we perfectly coin.

Blossoms in a Gentle Breeze

Flowers giggle in the springtime air,
Waving their petals without a care.
One cheeky bloom shouts, "Watch me dance!"
While bees crash in, like, "Give us a chance!"

A daisy jokes, "Why so serious, Rose?"
"Life's a garden party, strike a pose!"
Petals flutter, making hats and bows,
As we prance like squirrels, everyone knows.

With breezes tickling our colorful heads,
We bounce like bunnies in cozy beds.
Love in the garden is a riotous spree,
Where even the weeds join our jubilee.

So let's toss confetti made of green grass,
In this whimsical realm, we'll forever amass.
Together we bloom in this floral parade,
In laughter and petals, our hearts unafraid.

The Ethereal Wrap of Union

Two sweaters knitted in a tangled mess,
All tangled up in a soft, fuzzy stress.
We wear each other like a silly gown,
While the cat curls up like a royal crown.

In this patchwork quilt of bright, goofy squares,
We share chocolate kisses and mustardy glares.
Slipping on socks that are two sizes too small,
Our footsteps are whispers, or a loud guffaw.

We're two odd socks in a laundry spin,
Fighting static cling and a whirl through thin.
Love's a cyclone, whirling about,
With laughs that erupt, and a hearty shout.

In the embrace of threads, we find our way,
Stitched together in a comical play.
When tangled in each other, it's clear and true,
Life's like a sweater, meant for two.

A Cloud of Caring

Floating on air like a fluffy old chair,
A cloud of caring is everywhere.
With rain that giggles and sunshine that beams,
Love is a pillow, filled with sweet dreams.

Thunder rolls in with a funny old face,
"I'm here to rumble, just checking the space!"
But hugs from the sun, they warm up the scene,
As rainbows pop up, all shiny and keen.

We drift through the sky, like marshmallows bold,
Tickling the stars, laughing, uncontrolled.
Fluffy like whipped cream, we swirl and we sway,
Creating a masterpiece of playful ballet.

In this cloud of caring, let giggles cascade,
As we float through the laughter that never will fade.
Love's an airy treasure, making our hearts sing,
Floating together, let's spread our soft wings.

Hairpin Curves of Euphoria

Twists and turns, oh what a ride,
In your arms, I giggle and glide.
Like socks in a dryer, we spin around,
In this wild dance, joy's the only sound.

With heartbeats racing, we tackle the bends,
In laughter and chaos, our journey blends.
We zigzag through moments, so carefree and bright,
Holding you close, it feels just right.

The Gentle Fortress of Love

Cushy walls made of tickles and grins,
Defending our hearts from the world's whims.
We build forts with pillows, blankets galore,
And laugh till our tummies can't take anymore.

Every glance exchanged, a giggle ignites,
In our fortress of fun, joy takes flight.
With silly conversations and playful debates,
Love's the shield that humor creates.

Warm Embers of Intimacy

Like marshmallows roasting on a cool night,
S'mores and soft whispers, the moments feel right.
Our hearts crackle gently, embers of glee,
As we cuddle and laugh, just you and me.

With witty remarks and pokes here and there,
We keep love alight, in this cozy lair.
In the glow of our banter, sweet warmth is found,
In this charmed little bubble, we're blissfully bound.

Trails of Soft Laughter

On paths paved with giggles, we wander and stroll,
With chuckles that sparkle, we play our role.
In the woods of our silly, we skip and we prance,
With every footstep, we deepen our dance.

The echoes of glee are our compass and guide,
With you by my side, it feels like a ride.
Through trails of soft laughter, our hearts intertwine,
In this wacky adventure, forever you'll shine.

Soft Petals of Heartfelt Connection

In a world where socks do stray,
I found your heart, hip-hip-hooray!
You laugh at me when I trip,
But catch my fall with every slip.

Chocolate crumbs on my shirt,
You say I'm the sweetest dessert.
We dance like fools, in the rain,
Our love's a funny little game.

You steal my fries, I take your drink,
In this sweet madness, we don't think.
Each silly joke brings giggles bright,
In our plush blanket fort of delight.

With heart-shaped pancakes on a plate,
We toast to love—it's never late.
Like fuzzy socks in winter's chill,
Together, we fit, just like we will.

Murmurs of Sweet Solitude

In a quiet room, I laugh with glee,
Your snorts of joy are music to me.
We share our snacks, the popcorn flies,
As we both laugh till we tear our eyes.

Whispers of jokes dance on the floor,
Your quirky humor brings me more.
We puzzle pieces, mismatched yet great,
In our crazy world, we celebrate.

Silly antics, a plump little cat,
Sits on your lap, we're squished—how 'bout that?
We snuggle close, but dreams take flight,
In our world of giggles, everything's right.

Sip coffee strong, we toast the sun,
In this quirky life, we've already won.
With every sigh and every tease,
In this sweet solitude, we find our ease.

A Cocoon of Beloved Moments

Wrapped in laughter, a soft embrace,
Each silly story, we try to chase.
We giggle loud whenever we fall,
The world seems better—after all!

Your sock puppet talks with a silly squawk,
Together we weave our own brand of talk.
With every pun and every jest,
In this cocoon, we find our best.

Chasing rainbows on a Tuesday noon,
On rainy days, we sing a tune.
Your quirks are gems, they light the way,
In this love cocoon, we laugh and play.

Hand in hand, we stroll down the street,
In the parade of life, you're my best feat.
Through thick and thin, side by side,
In our little world, we always slide.

Embracing the Essence of Us

In mismatched shoes, we stroll along,
You hum that tune, oh so wrong!
With clumsy grace, we trip and twirl,
In this wild dance, let life unfurl.

You tease my dreams with silly quotes,
In this life boat, we're both the goats.
How we giggle, the echoes ring,
The essence of us is a funny thing!

Picnic blankets and snacks galore,
We fight for chips, but love's the score.
With winks and nudges, we share the fun,
In our playful universe, we've already won!

When the sun sets on our jolly spree,
You whisper, "You're a goofball to me."
With hearts wide open and laughter clear,
In this embrace, we hold each dear.

Silken Threads of Desire

I found your socks, they're softer than fleece,
Your humor wraps me—it's a warm release.
In tangled sheets, we play a silly game,
Your laughter's the yarn, and I'm wild for the fame.

We dance like cats on a sunbeam's delight,
You stole my fries—I won't start a fight!
In our cozy nook, I trip on your shoe,
Every moment with you feels joyously new.

The coffee's brewing, you take a big gulp,
With cream on your nose, what a charming sulk!
You tease me with puns, oh, what a sly wink,
In our loving circus, we're tighter than ink.

With playful quips, we bicker and jest,
Each silly spat brings out our very best.
So here's to the threads that weave as we spin,
In this frolic of love, let the laughter begin.

Warmth Wrapped in Serenity

A blanket burrito, you snuggle me tight,
Your hot cocoa breath warms the chilly night.
We melt as we giggle about silly things,
In our padded fortress, let the joy bells ring.

Your quirky dance moves, how they make me grin,
A clumsy pirouette that just might win.
Wrapped up in laughter, we both lose our way,
Finding joy in the chaos, come what may.

I bring you the popcorn, you spill it with glee,
In this love movie, who needs an Emmy?
We laugh at the dramas that sometimes unfold,
In your warm embrace, I feel never cold.

So here's to the cuddles, the giggles that pop,
Each little moment makes my heart flip-flop.
We're two joyful silly geese, won't trade it for gold,
Your warmth is my treasure, a story retold.

Lullabies of Heartfelt Connection

In soft whispers shared, our secrets collide,
Like kittens at play, with no need to hide.
You tickle my ribs, and I burst into fits,
In our realm of chuckles, love truly sits.

We trade goofy grins like kids in a park,
You slide down the banister, breaking the dark.
The lullabies hum as we dance in the night,
Our hearts weave a melody, pure and light.

We sway to the rhythm of silly delights,
Making pancakes together, what culinary fights!
Your spatula skills, oh my—what a show,
In our kitchen arena, love's laughter will flow.

Through bedtime shenanigans, dreams filled with fun,
Slice of cake in hand, hey, we're never done!
With lullabies soft, let the giggles resound,
In this world of wonders, our joy will abound.

Velvet Touch of Togetherness

Your velvet soft hugs, oh, they're never too tight,
We bumble through life, but it feels just right.
Our inside jokes land like snowflakes in June,
With whimsy and warmth, let's hum a sweet tune.

The cat's in the box, playing hide and seek,
As we roll on the floor, love's silly peak.
With cookie dough fights and flour in the air,
Each moment we share, I really don't care.

Your smile's like sunshine on my gloomy days,
It brightens my world in the funniest ways.
So take my hand now, let's leap and we'll dive,
In a sea of laughter, our spirits alive.

With you by my side, the mundane's a treat,
In this dance of connection, it's you I'll repeat.
So here's to life's velvet, its giggles and gleam,
Our beautiful story—a blissful daydream.

Silk Roads of the Heart

In a world of fluffy clouds,
I tripped on my heartstrings.
Puppies dance with giggles,
As the telephone sings.

Chocolate sprinkles on my toes,
Who knew love was a treat?
An octopus in a tuxedo,
Tap-dancing on my street.

Jellybeans spin pirouettes,
While rainbows paint the sky.
A love that's sweet as syrup,
Makes the waltzing fireflies fly.

Caught in a kitten's snare,
As I tumble in the grass.
With clowns juggling my fears,
How can this moment pass?

The Embrace of Kindred Spirits

In laughter's gentle grip,
We sail on bubbles high.
Nutty squirrels in tuxedos,
Twirl beneath the pie.

Dancing with rubber chickens,
In the garden of delight.
Hearts stitched with silly string,
Twinkling in the night.

Giggly ghosts in the rafters,
Whispering in my ear.
With balloons that have opinions,
And unicorns that cheer.

A waltz with jelly donuts,
Underneath the gleam.
We've crafted our own circus,
Living in a dream.

Cloud Nine Serenade

A love that tickles from on high,
Like feathers in the air.
Silly hats and bright balloons,
We float without a care.

Twirling on a bouncy castle,
Made of cotton candy.
Chasing after giggles,
With a sprinkle of dandy.

Whipped cream clouds dodge the stars,
As laughter takes its flight.
Dancing on a rainbow's spine,
We glow with pure delight.

And in a whirlwind's embrace,
We spin like tops in glee.
Love's a rib-tickling clown,
Oh, come and dance with me!

A Soft Serenade in the Night

Moonlight beams on silly dreams,
Where penguins play the flute.
Tickling toads in pajamas,
Fetch a rhyming suit.

Wrapped in whispers of delight,
We toast marshmallows bright.
Frogs with crowns lead the way,
To a funky nightlife.

Snuggling up with giggling stars,
That wink with playful light.
Every snore a melody,
As we dance through the night.

With love in goofy antics,
A serenade so sweet.
In a world of silly wonders,
Our hearts tap out the beat.

Doodles of Us

Your giggles bounce like rubber balls,
While I doodle hearts on bathroom walls.
With every wink, a mischief stirs,
We paint our world with silly blurs.

In mismatched socks we take our stand,
You wave your arms, I'm in command.
We dance like penguins, it's quite a sight,
Love's a circus, and we're the light!

With cookies crumbling on the floor,
You steal my fries, I shout, "No more!"
Yet in the chaos, we're a team,
Our jumbled lives, a perfect dream.

So let's embrace this crazy ride,
With laughter echoing far and wide.
In every blunder, we'll stay amused,
With all our moments, forever fused.

Tides of Tenderness

We ride the waves of silly games,
Like surfing cats with quirky names.
A sea of smiles, we splash and play,
Floating on whimsy every day.

You giggle like bubbles in the sun,
While I trip over, but it's all in fun.
Our love's a dance on sandy shores,
With footprints left, and laughter roars.

As tides come in, we lose our sting,
Building castles made of silly things.
We paddle deep, in silly glee,
Every tide holds warmth, you see.

So let our riptide sweep us away,
In a whirl of joy, we'll brightly sway.
With salty kisses and sandy feet,
Our playful hearts will ever beat.

Golden Threads of Togetherness

With yarn of laughs, we stitch and weave,
In patches bright, no room to grieve.
A quilt of quirks wrapped tight around,
In our cozy nook, pure joy is found.

Your puns and jests, like golden threads,
We laugh 'til we can't, laying in beds.
Each failure, a step in our quilted dance,
A tapestry woven in silly romance.

With mismatched pillows and tea-stained cups,
You snort with laughter as I spill my ups.
In every stitch, a memory glows,
Our golden bonds are how love grows.

So let's knit our dreams through every seam,
In this bumpy ride, we're a team.
With warmth and charm, we greet each day,
In silly harmony, we'll always play.

Serenity in Sweet Invitations

With cupcakes and chaos, we paint the scene,
You call me over, and I'm feeling keen.
A picnic blanket spread underneath the sun,
With ice cream spills, our outing's begun!

You whisper secrets in chocolate sauce,
While I pretend I'm a friendly horse.
In little games, we toss the bread,
Sharing smiles, as the ducks are fed.

The art of jest in every bite,
You steal my dessert, what a delight!
With every giggle, our hearts grow bold,
In this sweet unity, life unfolds.

So join me now, let laughter reign,
In this joyful feast, we'll never wane.
With sweet invitations and funny flair,
We're the perfect pair, beyond compare!

Charms of Softness

In a blanket fort we hide,
Making giggles our guide.
With popcorn storms and a sneeze,
You laugh while I say, "Please!"

Whipped cream fights on the floor,
You're sticky; I want more.
With every hug, I just can't stop,
Your smile makes my heart pop!

Tacos tossed like paper planes,
Our love's a dance on silly trains.
In every snort and silly grin,
I see the joy you wrap me in.

So let's chase clouds and pretend,
That each day is a game to bend.
With laughter loud and hearts so bright,
We'll stay cuddled, day and night.

Trails of Serenaded Souls

We dance like squirrels in the trees,
Your laugh's a tune upon the breeze.
With twirls that make no sense at all,
  Our hearts collide, we trip and fall.

Ice cream dribbles down your chin,
  A chocolate smile, we both grin.
Lost in the mess of what we create,
You take my hand; it feels just great.

  Whispers shared by candlelight,
You say my jokes are quite the sight.
With rolling eyes, you tease me near,
  While I serenade you, don't you fear!

Each moment's funny, wildly sweet,
  In every mishap, love's a treat.
So let's wander through this delight,
  You and I, an endless flight.

Plum Blossom Dreams

In gardens where the blossoms sway,
We stitch our dreams in shades of gray.
With giggling petals flying free,
You chase a bee that's chasing me.

Each hiccup sounds like music's song,
You say it can't take too long.
With each fruit fall that hits our heads,
We laugh 'til jelly's spread in beds.

Our hearts bloom like springtime flowers,
Amid the dance of silly hours.
With every chuckle, we both grow,
These fruity dreams, they steal the show.

So here's to fun's ever-bright scheme,
With you, my love, what a sweet dream!
In every smirk, in every twist,
We find the joy, we can't resist.

Moonlit Caress

Under stars that twinkle bright,
You trip on air, what a sight!
With every blush, you steal my breath,
In laughter, we dance with no death.

The moon's a spotlight on our game,
We're trying not to say your name.
With funny faces, secrets share,
In the night breeze, without a care.

Silly shadows chase our feet,
Together making night's heart beat.
In each embrace, we softly blend,
You're my partner, my silly friend.

So let's waltz these silver beams,
In our world full of dreams.
With whispers and chuckles, we will sail,
In this night, our love won't fail.

Hug of the Heart

In the squishy realm of cuddly cheer,
Where hugs are found without any fear.
A good squeeze here, a tickle there,
Laughter dances in the cozy air.

With bear-like arms, I'm soft and bold,
In this embrace, we both feel gold.
Funny faces as we twist and bend,
Who knew love could make us pretend?

Like marshmallows melting in a warm cup,
We fumble and tumble, never give up.
Our giggles echo, our joy's a blast,
Wrapped up like burritos, we laugh so fast.

So let's embrace in this silly way,
Where love's a game we play all day.
With every chuckle, our hearts collide,
In a hug so tight, our worries slide.

Valleys of Velvet Intentions

In valleys deep of plush delight,
Where hearts explore by day and night.
A pillow fight, oh what a scene,
Laughter springs forth, like a trampoline.

Over cushions, we bounce and soar,
Velvet dreams where we can explore.
There's no such thing as 'too much fun',
Our silly antics weigh a ton!

In a whisper, I'll share my snack,
You take a bite, then watch my back.
With glee, we munch, our crumbs take flight,
On this merry carpet, everything's right!

So here we float in giddy bliss,
Each hug's a whirl, a merry twist.
With warmth as thick as peanut spread,
In these valleys, let's never dread!

Quiet Echoes of Togetherness

In cozy corners where whispers play,
We share our dreams in a silly way.
With quiet echoes, our secrets bloom,
Like bubble wrap popping in a room.

While sipping tea, my hand in yours,
We giggle softly, open the doors.
With muffled laughs as we share a grin,
It feels like magic, where else to begin?

In our giggly haven, we pull the light,
As silly shadows dance with delight.
Your snort's my favorite sound tonight,
In every moment, everything feels right.

So let's whisper plans for our next quest,
In this bubble of love, we are truly blessed.
With each small chortle, our hearts connect,
In echoes soft, our love's perfect.

Dreamy Echoes of a Whispered Promise

Amidst the pillows, dreams take flight,
We giggle gently into the night.
With whispered promises, oh what a scene,
Like two silly kids, in a dream machine.

Your cheeky grin makes my heart race,
We share our hiccups and dream of space.
Twinkling stars in this goofy plan,
Together we'll leap, frolic and span.

In whispered tones, adventures unfold,
Like treasure maps of bright, good gold.
Each giggle echoes, an endless song,
In these sweet dreams, we both belong.

So let's keep laughing, still in our cocoon,
With hearts so light, like a balloon.
In a funny world where we sketch our fate,
Our dreams align, oh isn't that great?